It is Freezing

by Rachel Russ
Illustrated by Bill Ledger

OXFORD
UNIVERSITY PRESS

In this story ...

Pip

Pip is strong.
She can lift rocks.

Ben

Jin

Slink

It is freezing.
Pip needs her coat.

3

This is loads of fun!

trail

Ben runs fast.

Ben cannot push it.
He stops and groans.

It is
too big.

Pip is strong. She can push it.

Jin sighs.
He cannot lift it.

It is not light!

Pip is strong.
She can lift it up high.

Is it a man?

Pip gets three bits of coal.

pat
pat
pat

Jin picks up six twigs.

It needs a tail.

A tail? Is it a dog?

12

Retell the story ...